This Workbook Belongs To:

_____

Published by Happie Face Publishing Company, 2019

Copyright © 2019 Mark Corbin

All rights reserved.

ISBN: 978-0-9994726-8-2

Table of Contents

Letter to the Friends of Mark ………………………………………………………..… 4

Igniters and Inhibitors Explained …………………………………………………...….. 6

Discover Your Power Tools - The Paramount 5 ……………………………………...… 7

Power Tool – Discovery ……………………………………………………………...… 8

Power Tools for your Success - Get to It! ……………………………………………… 9

Life List © …………………………………………………………………………..… 10

Power Tool 1 - Purpose Inhibitors ……………………………………………………. 12

Power Tool - S.M.A.R.T Victory ……………………………………………………… 18

Power Tool 2 - Drive Inhibitors ………………………………………………………. 20

Power Tool - Keep Going! …………………………………………………………… 24

Power Tool - Dream Killers …………………………………………………………... 27

Power Tool 3 - Passion Inhibitors …………………………………………………….. 30

Power Tool – Visualize ……………………………………………………………….. 34

Power Tool 4 - Patience Inhibiters ……………………………………………………. 36

Power Tool – Believe …………………………………………………………………. 39

Power Tool - You Need to Get ………………………………………………………... 40

Power Tool 5 – Perseverance …………………………………………………………. 41

Bonus Content: Power Tools Weekly Planner ………………………………...……… 47

Notes ………………………………………………………………………………..… 57

Sources ……………………………………………………………………………..… 60

Friends:

I have concluded that if you can identify the people, places, or things that **inhibit** your forward progress or cause you to pause, then I believe you can overcome any obstacle to your personal success in life.

Likewise, if you can identify memories, people, places, or things that **ignite** your forward progress then there is nothing that can hold you back from becoming the person you dreamed you would be when you were a child.

I pray that you find this workbook useful in moving you forward within a world that is so desperately in need of you, your gifts, and your unique skills.

Mark Corbin

"Success requires action; by taking action, you can change your life!"

· Mark Corbin ·

Power Tools for Your Success
Igniters and Inhibitors

Before we get started, allow me to introduce two terms that you will encounter in this workbook: **igniters** and **inhibitors.**

For this workbook, we will define **igniters** and **inhibitors** in the following manner:

Igniters can be a person, a place, and a thing that provides mental motivation and allow you to move forward.

You will uncover and confront your **inhibitors**.

Inhibitors are obstacles or people, places, things and events that cause you to hesitate or stop and can evoke a general feeling of fear and reluctance. Inhibitors may come in the form of doubt, a place or an oppressive environment, or a negative person.

You will come to understand how to free yourself from your **inhibitors**.

Heed these warnings:
- Motivation is key but let's add some clarity to what motivation is:
- The word motivation stems from the Latin word "movere" which means to move. Your motivation level is what moves you to participate in an activity and it affects your desire to continue the activity.
- *Power Tools for Your Success* will help you develop the discipline to help you create new strength to keep you on the path to your personal growth and success.
- Be careful about using a person or people as an igniter. Men and women's feet slip when placed in high places, so protect yourself against idol worship.
- Do not give too much credit to those people who have impacted your life negatively; perhaps they have had too much power yover our lives, but now it is time to take back your power.

#PowerTools4Success

Discover Your Power Tools
The Paramount 5

1. **Purpose:** To set as an aim, intention, or goal for oneself.

2. **Drive:** To strive vigorously toward a goal or objective and with determination.

3. **Perseverance:** Steady persistence in a course of action despite difficulties, obstacles, or discouragement.

4. **Patience:** Endurance, grit, calm, stability, and courage in demanding circumstances.

5. **Passion:** The state of being acted upon or affected by something external, especially something foreign to one's nature.

Power Tool
Discovery

Why Do You Do What You Do? For a while now, you have been going about your life from assignment to assignment, job to job, and in some cases, relationship to relationship with mediocre results.

To help you overcome your **inhibitor (s)** or to discover your **igniter (s)** there is a series of discovery questions you must answer, starting with why do you do what you do?

Now, answer the question with the intention that you will overcome all that hinders you and knowing that someone who has your back.

Cut through the life stuff, relationship and lies you have been told and began to believe about yourself and get to the real answers about who, what, and why you are the person you have become. As you answer, focus on where you have been.

Look at those areas in your life, as they have been used to mold you into the person you are and are about to become.

_____

_____

_____

_____

I would like to hear from you. If you find yourself unable to find any answers, contact me via Facebook Messenger at mcpowertools@gmail.com and let's work together or find the best resources to help you grow.

Notes:

_____

_____

_____

Power Tools for Your Success
Your Change Starts with You!

I will share a lot of the touchy-feely things you and I are probably accustomed to when reading personal development books and here is why:

1. **Time is running out**—neither you nor I have an abundance of time to figure out the requirements to get us from the place we find ourselves in now and into the place where we are destined to be. Do not put off the change you desire for your life one more day. Stop repeating the mantra, "There is always tomorrow." That could be true, but why wait to be happy if happy is what you want to be?

2. **We have done enough talking**. Now is the time to elevate our minds, bodies, and spirits to the next level. There is nothing else left to say that hasn't been said or thought a thousand times before. This is your life and as you stand here looking over into the precipice, decide what it is you are seeing. Are you looking forward to "a life of love and a world of joy," or a bottomless pit of despair? I don't know about you, but I choose "a life of love and a world of joy."

This is your life and our paths have crossed at this time because you have decided that you are not living the life you want. So, let's change it. It can be done; all you must do is make up your mind.

Making up your mind is a daily exercise. Yes, I have discovered that even on my best days, the negative energy seeps into my mind. This is a battle that you can win, but it requires discipline, and you will learn how to create the pattern for disciplined success in this workbook.

#PowerTools4Success

Power Tools
Life List©

Create a Life List© of all the accomplishments you have had until this point in your life. Next, create a list of things you want to complete before your life is over. From time to time, we will refer back to your Life List to assist with other pages within this workbook.

Life Up Until Now	What I am Going to Do
1.	1.
2.	2.
3.	3.
4	4
5.	5.
6.	6.
7.	7.
8.	8.
9.	9.
10.	10.
11.	11.
12.	12.
13.	13.
14.	14.
15.	15.
16.	16.
17.	17.
18.	18.
19.	19.
20.	20.
21.	21.
22.	22.
23.	23.
24	24
25.	25.
26.	26.
27.	27.
28.	28.
29.	29.
30.	30.

Power Tools
Life List ©

Use this space to reflect on your **Life List** © and why you have waited until now to pursue so many things. The goal of this exercise is to help you visually (write) confront the obstacles that have stood in your path to the life you desire. The key to this exercise is that JUST WRITE.

[Note: the only way to do poorly with this list is not to write anything. JUST WRITE and *Keep writing.]*

Power Tool 1
Purpose Inhibitors

Purpose: To set as an aim, intention, or goal for oneself.

Why are you at this place and why do you think you are stuck? I have read many personal development books that talk about why people are stuck in their "situations." Through my own experiences driven by poor decisions and unwillingness to change, I too have felt that I was trapped in some never-ending loop of mediocrity and failure. As I searched for a way out of the loop of backwardness, it was not until I talked with my friend, Leroy Miles, who I believe by far gave me the best answer to the question. His answer was rather succinct. He said, *"90% of can't is won't."* That one answer was enough at the time to help push me to change how I was living. Oddly enough I needed to hear that at the time, and I get that.

It is not always that we can't change our lives, but a lot of times we won't because we just can't see the other side of the change. One of my purposes for the Power Tools Workbook is to provide clarity of your vision.

So here we go:

One of the first things that I decided was to figure out what things inhibited me from making change. I knew that changes needed to be made, but I was not willing to confront the lies I was telling myself along with this self-imposed fear that I was not smart or good enough that had me unable to move. As each day passed, I realized that I was inhibiting my personal growth.

Imagine knowing that everything you want is on the other side of a door and to get what you want; all you need do is open the door. The problem is you spend so much time trying to figure out whether the door is locked, what the door is made of, or if you will get hurt if you touch the door. You waste time finding reasons not to move when all you need to do is open the door. That's right - all you need to do is step forward, grab the knob, turn the knob and push the door open.

Turning the knob was difficult for me to do and trust and believe I know for some of us it will be just as or even more difficult to do, but the door can be opened by YOU.

All you need to do is grab the doorknob and open.

Power Tool 1
Purpose • Inhibitors

The number **#1 inhibitor:** *YOU*.

Confronting yourself can be Herculean task and it was a struggle for me to literally look at myself in the mirror and talk to me about who and what I had become. I was not proud of who I became, but I knew I needed to change.

If change is what you want, you can do it and together we can work on a new pathway for your future:

1. The first step in the process of overcoming "won't" is deciding to change and not turning back.

2. The second step is easy; To achieve it, all you need to do is place **won't** in your Power Tools for Success Toolbox. It would be easy to tell you to throw the old memories away, but the fact of the matter is they never go away. Placing the old failure, mistake, lies and betrayals in the Power Tools Tool Box gives you the ability to know where your stuff is and gives you the ability to understand that the only way those things can come out is that you purposely bring them out. Yes, you can look into the Toolbox, but don't you dare pick anything up.

3. Make a **won't** list and be sure your list includes those things that have hindered you throughout your life such as: indecisiveness, letting her go or let him go, seeking help for an addiction, etc. Only you know your **won't** and you and only you must put the **won't** in the **Power Tools Toolbox**.

    We are at the beginning stages of change and our focus from here on out is on what you will do and what you won't do for your personal growth and success.

Now, in the space below, let's deal with your other **purpose inhibitors:** What three inhibitors have you encountered in your life that you believe have held back your success?

1. People: _____
2. Places: _____
3. Things: _____

Identify your **inhibitors** and let's create a plan to grow beyond the limitations you have placed upon you.

Power Tool 1
Purpose Inhibitors • Workspace

We are on the verge of change. Change is interesting because when all you do is talk about it, all obstacles seem to sit still and never move. However, when you move towards change, change can appear to be massive. I embrace change in action in the pattern of W. Clement Stone, who once said, "Thinking will not overcome fear, but action will." It is time to overcome the fear(s) of what lies beyond your comfort zone and attack the world that has been holding your freedom hostage.

Attacking and defeating your fears will require you to get comfortable with being uncomfortable. As you will discover, in order to have more, you will need to do more than you have ever done before you can align your life with your **purpose.**

In the space below, write the things you have not wanted to deal with and confront them on paper. Getting out of your comfort zone and growing your abilities builds courage, discipline, and ushers in change. Begin with admitting to yourself the things you don't want to do but must do to free yourself.

_____
_____
_____
_____
_____
_____
_____
_____
_____
_____

Power Tool 1
Purpose Igniters

Having now defined **purpose,** let us focus on the things that **ignite** your passions, motivate you to move forward, and those things that make you jump out of the bed and run into your day. In this section, you will uncover your **purpose igniters**.

In the space below, consider your **purpose igniters** and list **three igniters** that are the source of your inspiration. Spend a few minutes thinking about it this way: In your worst-case scenario, if you lost everything that you owned and cared for, what would it take to encourage you to get moving again, to earn, to win and to fight to take everything back?

1. _____

2. _____

3. _____

Now is the time to light a fire under your ambitions and pursue them with all your strength.

List three things from your **Life List** © that you have not shared with anyone below. Select a want, a need, and something you just must to have. These are things that you have been reluctant to pursue out of fear, lack of confidence, or fear of what others would say or think about you. STOP BEING AFRAID. All of creation is waiting on you to share your gifts with the world.

1. Want: _____

2. Need: _____

3. Must Have: _____

"Trust yourself. Create the kind of self that you will be happy to live with all your life. Make the most of yourself by fanning the tiny; inner sparks of possibility into flames of achievement." – Golda Meir

Power Tool 1
Purpose Life Components

Purpose is difficult to decipher without major life components. During this phase of growth, what I learned was that focus is key. Specifically, my focus had to be on developing knowledge, financial, and fitness/health growth plans. Each of the other components is important, but the health plan is paramount. I realized that without good health, the components would not matter. At one point, I was 326 pounds and knew that if I did not fix my health, earning and having money would be nice but I would not be around to spend it. Consider the following components:

Knowledge	Financial	Physical Fitness
Month 1: What will you learn: Identify a Source: Goal of Learning:	**Month 1:** What will you learn: Identify a Source: Goal of Saving:	**Month 1:** What will you learn: Identify a Source: Goal of Fitness:
Month 2: What will you learn: Identify a Source: Goal of Learning:	**Month 2:** What will you learn: Identify a Source: Goal of Saving:	**Month 2:** What will you learn: Identify a Source: Goal of Fitness:
Month 3: What will you learn: Identify a Source: Goal of Learning:	**Month 3:** What will you learn: Identify a Source: Goal of Saving:	**Month 3:** What will you learn: Identify a Source: Goal of Fitness:

It is important that you commit to gaining new knowledge in this period of change in your life. Educate yourself. To have a distinct advantage over your competition , read and learn. **#PowerTools4Success**

Power Tool 1
Purpose Igniters • Workspace

How indispensable do you want to become? When I started my first job out of college, my first manager told me, "Always be associated with a task nobody else can do." Well, what task are you going to be associated with that nobody else can do? Write it down. **#PowerTools4Success**

Power Tool 2
S.M.A.R.T. Victory

Through my own struggles, I believe each one of us needs a daily S.M.A.R.T Victory to boost our self-esteem, courage, and belief in ourselves. You have seen the **S.M.A.R.T.** acronym before, but for our purposes, **S.M.A.R.T.** stands for **S: Specific** (the What, Why, and How), **M: Measurable** (if you can't measure it, you can't manage it), **A: Attainable** (create a clear picture in your mind of what you want. Your mind and perseverance will figure out ways you can make them happen.), **R: Realistic** (doable), and **T: Timely** (set a timeframe for achieving your goal. You must be date-specific, i.e. December 1, 2020). The matrix below will help with preparing your **S.M.A.R.T. Victory.**

Start	Start your week with a specific goal in mind. **Specific** is the **what, why,** and **how.** Do you want to get in better physical condition or learn a new skill? **Sunday** is your planning day. Begin your Sunday with gratitude. Next, think of your goals for the week ahead. Then at 5:00 p.m., make a list of your goals for the week ahead. Before you go to bed, write your goals and let them marinate in your mind while you sleep. As Monday dawns, you will be mentally prepared to focus on your achievements for the week ahead.
Whatever it Takes	There may be obstacles in your way each day. Obstacles are also **measurable** and remember—If you **can't measure it, you can't manage it.** It may require you to bend over backward in order to accomplish your desired task and you will do so. At this stage of the game, you may already know what some obstacles are, and when they will appear, plan for them, get around them, and move on.
Beat it to Death	You will have to beat some old habits to death and bury them to attain your goals. Start with an **inhibitor funeral** – on a strip of paper, write all your **progress inhibitors**, then lay the strip of paper on your desk and sweep it into the trash. The funeral is over. To attain your goals, get a clear picture in your mind of what you want, and your mind, body, and spirit will figure out ways you can make it happen.
Carry it No Further	You will have to carry some of your old junk into this new week but only as long as it takes to read this sentence. Believe that what you want to achieve is realistic for **you.** This is about *you* and what *you* think is realistic, not about what those around you think is "doable". You have done your research and you know what you are doing. There will be those who say, "I can't see you making that happen." Keep the words of my sister, Carmen, in mind: "Maybe it isn't for them to see!" Move on from people-pleasing and "performance love." Drop it.
Finish Strong	You have made your plan, written your plan, and now it's time to work your plan. To ensure your **S.M.A.R.T. Victory,** set a time for achieving your goal. Be date and time-specific–for example, 11:00 a.m. on January 1, 2020. *Congratulations in* advance for each victory that you have won this week through faith, focus, and perseverance. Go look at your smiling face in the mirror and remember the feelings you have. It feels good and it will continue to feel good as long you focus on the **S.M.A.R.T. Victory. Get to it.**

Power Tool
S.M.A.R.T. Victory • Template

Use this **S.M.A.R.T. Victory** template to prepare yourself for the week ahead. Remember to use all the elements for the **S.M.A.R.T. Victory** to ensure your success:

S: Specific: What, Why, and How
M: Measurable: If you can't measure it, you can't manage it
A: Attainable: Picture what it is you want, and your mind and perseverance will figure out ways you can make it/them happen.
R: Realistic: "doable"
T/Timely: Set a timeframe for achieving your goal. Be time and date-specific i.e. December 1, 2020.

Let me know how your first week goes at ***mcpowertools@gmail.com.***

Start	(S): Specific:
Whatever it Takes	(M): Measurable:
Beat it to Death	(A): Attainable:
Carry it No Further	(R): Realistic:
Finish Strong	(T): Timely:

I know you have been fighting and struggling to remain relevant, and some days it gets just downright tough to even put one foot in front of the other. I want you to know you can get through this – stay faithful and pray!

Power Tool 2
Drive

DRIVE: To strive vigorously toward a goal or objective and with determination.

"Go hard," "Max-Out," "Give 110%," and "Be all that you can be," are all great slogans, but are they a way to live your life? I have used them all, but as I enter this stage of my life, I am sure that a good slogan, by itself isn't enough. It's funny how you can go through life knowing things about you but be unwilling to accept them as truth. In my case, I had known something for a while but was unsure of the cause and effect until recently when I attended the Enon Tabernacle Baptist Men's Retreat. While at the retreat, Pastor Waller asked a simple question, "What happened to you?" It was at that moment that all the other things I had been holding back appeared before my eyes.

Now, I want to ask you that same question - *what happened to you?* Only you know the answer to the question. Think about the event or the person who came into your life or left you and caused you to fade, hideout or just plain disappear from your life.

So, before we delve further into your **drive**, I want you to take a few moments to pinpoint when, what, and who you allowed to hinder your **drive**:

1. What: _____
2. Who: _____
3. When: _____

Review what you have written above and then give yourself permission to let all of it go! The damage caused and the control that you have allowed others to exert over your life **ceases right now!**

It's time to take your life back. I would like to suggest that you use this Ralph Waldo Emerson quote as part of your daily motivation, "What we fear doing the most is usually most what we need to do."

Now that you have dealt with those **drive inhibitors**, I want you to repeat this: *It is not too late for you to become the person you dreamt of becoming when you were a child!* **#PowerTools4Success**

Power Tool 2
Drive Inhibitors

What **drives** you to be better each day? It is imperative that you understand what **drives** you to strive vigorously toward a goal or objective; to work, play, or try wholeheartedly and with determination. List three of your drivers in this space:

1. _____

2. _____

3. _____

Do not take this exercise for granted – you must be sure of your **drivers,** as you will need to grasp them tightly when the **inhibitors** raise their troublesome head and try to discourage or kill your drive.

In the space below, write your **drive inhibitors.** What three **inhibitors,** including people or places have encountered in your past and current life that you believe **inhibit** your success?

1. People: _____

2. Places: _____

3. Things: _____

Focus on what you believe to be your **drive inhibitors.** If your statement begins with "if only…" Refuse to get stuck on the "if only." **I believe you are about to become better than you have ever been!**

I want you to take this time to claim full responsibility for you and your actions. If you have allowed fear, threats, or the fear of loss to hold you back, now is the time for you to "stake your claim" to your life. This is your time to act and go in a new and positive direction.

Power Tool 2
Drive Inhibitors • Workspace

Take a moment and deal with the following question: "What or who happened to you?" Who hurt you? What happened that was so painful that you are no longer the individual you enjoyed being? Prayerfully, by the time you and I meet, I can tell you what happened to me and you can do the same. Write it down, deal with it on this page, and leave it here.

Power Tool 2
Drive Igniters

Now that we've started working through your **inhibitors,** it is time to hit something. What are your **drive igniters** – thoughts, things, and motivations that make you **strive vigorously toward a goal?** Now is not the time for you to say, "I don't know." My friend, *you* are the **hammer** and any obstacle on your path to success is a **nail** and you need to hit that nail as hard as you can! In the space below, list three of your **drivers**, i.e. spouse, children, money, power, etc. Only you know what drives you:

1. People: _____

2. Places: _____

3. Things: _____

In the space below, I would like for you to consider your **drive igniters:** List three igniters that are the source of your drive. Your **drive igniters** differ from your **purpose igniters**. Spend a few minutes thinking about it this way: When you were a child, what made you want to become the go after your dreams?

1. _____

2. _____

3. _____

Review your list. These are your **drive igniters**. You can still achieve all that you want, but you must discover the things that light a fire under you. **#PowerTools4Success**

Daily Power Tool
Quotes to Keep You Going!

"Today, you have 100% of your life left." – Tom Landry

"Action is a great restorer and builder of confidence. Inaction is not only the result but the cause of fear. Perhaps the action you take will be successful. Perhaps different action or adjustments will have to follow. But any action is better than no action at all." – Norman Vincent Peale

"Perfection is not attainable, but if we chase perfection, we can catch excellence." – Vince Lombardi

"There is nothing stronger than a woman who has rebuilt herself." Hannah Gadsby

"The moment you accept responsibility for everything in your life is the moment you gain the power to change anything in your life." Hal Elrod

"A man does what he must - in spite of personal consequences, in spite of obstacles and dangers and pressures - and that is the basis of all human morality." – Winston Churchill

"Continuous effort - not strength or intelligence - is the key to unlocking our potential." – Winston Churchill

"Have a bias toward action - let's see something happen now. You can break that big plan into small steps and take the first step right away." – Indira Gandhi

"Leadership is a matter of having people look at you and gain confidence, seeing how you react. If you're in control, they're in control." – Tom Landry

"Change is the law of life. And those who look only to the past or present are certain to miss the future." – John F. Kennedy

"Always bear in mind that your own resolution to succeed is more important than any other." – Abraham Lincoln

"If ignorant both of your enemy and yourself, you are certain to be in peril." – Sun Tzu

"Cast your burden on the LORD, And He shall sustain you; He shall never permit the righteous to be moved." – Psalm 55:22 (NKJV)

"You are not accidental. The world needs you. Without you something will be missing in existence and nobody can replace it." – Osho

"Most fears of rejection rest on the desire for approval from other people. Don't base your self-esteem on their opinions." – Harvey Mackay

Power Tool 2
Drive Igniters

To maintain your **drive power** and benefit from your **drive igniters**, you will need to be **fit!** For this workbook, we will use **fit** as an adjective, defined as suitable to meet the required purpose. To be fit for the required purpose, you must define your desired purpose.

1. Do you want to feel better?
2. Do you want your clothes to fit better?
3. Do you want to have enough stamina to spend time with your spouse and to play with your children?

Think about being fit this way. As the master of your home, you purchased a set of knives and since your purchase, the knives have remained in the kitchen drawer not being used. Finally, a year goes by and its Thanksgiving Day and you need a sharp knife. Suddenly, you remember the new knives in the drawer and pull out a knife only to find that its blade has become dull and cannot be used for its intended to purpose - to cut. You try to carve the turkey anyway, but you realize that your knives are not fit for the master's use.

Reflect on this: In your present level of fitness are you fit for the Master's use?

☐ Yes
☐ No

Answer this question: Are you ready to become the person you dreamt of becoming when you were a child? If yes, then who? If no, why not?

Power Tool 2
Drive • Workspace

Are you fit for the Master's use? Write what you must do first to become fit. Deal with everything from mental and dietary discipline. I had to give up cookies. What are you willing to give up, even for a short period of time, to get fit for the Master's use? **#PowerTools4Success**

Power Tool
Dream Killers

Beware of "dream killers" as they come in different shapes, sizes, and colors. Listed below are characterizations of how dream killers can appear. Learn to recognize your dream killers and stay vigilant in your daily pursuit of your goals.

Strategy Buster	Strategy Buster and his vile gang, the Distractions, will attempt to sabotage your plans daily. Keep in mind those disguised, as Strategy Busters have no superpowers. However, he will attempt to derail your plans with all sorts of last-minute glitches – showing up unexpectedly, not finishing their assignments, and other nefarious focus busters that are designed to drain your patience and energy.
Temptation	Nasty, sneaky Temptation has been gunning for you for as long as you can remember. Keep both eyes open for Temptation and its ability to change its physical appearance into the things you want most and need the least at the time when it shows up. You must always be alert, as we know Temptation is likely to show up when you get tired or when your mind wanders off its assigned task. Remember, your faith and integrity are the keys to beating Temptation.
The Doubt Squad	Also known as the "Miserable Comforters". They have done their homework, have studied you for long time, and sometimes, may resemble friends. However, you will know the "Miserable Comforters" as they make statements similar to, "What makes you think you can do that?" "You are too old to be starting a new career", or "Nobody will buy that from you." Their powers drain your confidence and are mood-altering, so keep your head up.

Once you can identify your enemies, learning to defeat them becomes exponentially less difficult. List your Dream Killers below and commit to defeating them.

(1)_____, (2) _____, (3) _____

#PowerTools4Success

Power Tool
Dream Killers – Defense

Self-Care is the key ingredient needed when fighting against your dream killers. There will be days when you will destroy them, but there will also be days when the best you can do is to hold your ground to defend yourself from further negative advancement against your goals.

Below are Power Tools that will be help combat the dream killers in your life:

1. **Find ways to relieve stress** – Exercise, practice yoga, or pray daily. You may have to do these things more frequently when times get tough.
2. **Create a Mastermind Group** – Mastermind groups offer a combination of brainstorming, accountability, and support in a small group setting. Consider meeting at least once a month in person or more often by text to stay on track with your goals and to assist your group members with theirs.
3. **Read a book** – Biographies are great. I recommend: *Why Should White Guys Have All the Fun? How Reginald Lewis Created a Billion-Dollar Business Empire* by Reginald F. Lewis, Hugh B. Price, and Blair S. Walker, *Feel the Fear and Do It Anyway* by Susan Jeffers and *Rising Strong* by Brene' Brown.
4. **Stop answering every call and every text** – You know not every call or every text is urgent.
5. **Enjoy your weekend** – Stop adding to your stress and leave work at work.
6. **Choose a time to answer emails** – Choose a time to answer your emails, either right before lunch or an hour before you depart work.
7. **Find a reason to laugh** – Allow **yourself** the ability to laugh out loud. Sounds strange, but for so long the best I could do is to say aloud, "that's funny." I've changed, and to be honest, some days there is nothing better than a good belly laugh.
8. **Stop chasing grown people** – I have relationships that only exist because I reach out to that person. I've decided that I no longer have the will to maintain one-sided relationships. You and I both deserve better from the people we allow in our lives than that. Don't let another day go by with you trying to figure out the importance of the relationship – it is not what you thought it was.

Power Tool
Dream Killers • Workspace

Dream killers are funny. I have come to understand that depending on your self-confidence, **dream killers** can resemble paper tigers. Paper tigers are people who tell you how great they are and promise that they can help you but don't deliver. No sooner than they open their mouths, you know they could not get it done. Who are the paper tigers in your life that you have to cut loose? No need to wait. Write the name(s) and leave it here. Remember, "Every rat looks like an elephant in a jungle filled with mice." **#PowerTools4Success**

Power Tool 3
Passion Inhibitors

PASSION: the state of being acted upon or affected by something external, especially something alien to one's nature.

What **inhibits** your passion?

List three (3) of your **passion inhibitors** in this space:

1. _____
2. _____
3. _____

Here's an example from the Bible to better explain. The Apostle Paul describes the "thorn in the flesh" in 2 Corinthians 12:7-10; "⁷ And lest I should be exalted above measure by the abundance of the revelations, a thorn in the flesh was given to me, a messenger of Satan to buffet me, lest I be exalted above measure. ⁸ Concerning this thing I pleaded with the Lord three times that it might depart from me. ⁹ And He said to me, "My grace is sufficient for you, for my strength is made perfect in weakness." Therefore most gladly I will rather boast in my infirmities, that the power of Christ may rest upon me. ¹⁰ Therefore I take pleasure in **infirmities, in reproaches, in needs, in persecutions, in distresses,** for Christ's sake. For when I am weak, then I am strong."

What are your infirmities, reproaches, needs, persecutions, and distresses? These are the external things or people alien to your nature that **inhibit** your passion. Paul listed five items and I would like for you to do the same to discover our **passion inhibitors**:

1. _____
2. _____
3. _____
4. _____
5. _____

We must deal with these external forces to get our passion(s) back on track.
#PowerTools4Success

Power Tool 3
Passion Inhibitor • Workspace

By now, you have realized that what ails most of us is the power we have allowed other people to have over our lives. We are not called to like each other, but we are charged to love your neighbor as yourself. The funny thing is, for a lot of us, we have not loved ourselves and that has made it difficult to love anyone else. Go get your passion back and go hard after your dreams. Do you have a "thorn in the flesh" that God's grace has helped you deal with? Describe it in the space below.

_____
_____
_____
_____
_____
_____
_____
_____
_____
_____
_____
_____
_____
_____
_____
_____
_____
_____

Power Tool 3
Passion Igniters

With passion defined, let us focus on the things that **ignite your passion**. What are the emotions, thoughts, and actions that make you want to step to the front of the line when volunteers are needed to solve a problem or to save your part of the world? **#PowerTools4Success**

A **passion igniter** can be a lesson you learned at the knee of your mom or dad, something you learned from a teacher, or just a good, but painful lesson you learned as an adult that makes you want to be the best you possible?

List three **passion igniters** that rest at the center of your passion:

1. _____
2. _____
3. _____

In case you are not sure what you are passionate about, here's an oldie but a goodie to shake your passion loose.

> *"What makes a King out of a slave?* **Courage!** *What makes the flag on the mast to wave?* **Courage!** *What makes the elephant charge his tusk in the misty mist or the dusky dusk!* **Courage!** *What makes the muskrat guard his musk?* **Courage!** *What makes the Sphinx the 7th Wonder?* **Courage!** *What makes the dawn come up like* **THUNDER!** **Courage!**" – the Cowardly Lion, from *The Wizard of Oz*

What causes your passion to rise? **Courage!** Be courageous!

Power Tool 3
Passion Igniters Workspace

In this space, **write your very own courage speech. #PowerTools4Success**

Power Tool
Visualize

It's time to "cast your vision" for the revitalized you! *Visualize* means **to form a mental image of**. Follow the next three steps very carefully:

1. Find an environment that is comfortable, quiet, and suitable for you to do some thinking.
2. Block out 15 to 30 minutes to sit and envision yourself achieving your goals.
3. Finally, write what you see in your mind's eye in the space below.

You are only to write the things you see *yourself* doing, not what others think you ought to be doing. It is time for us to move away from "performance love". Performance love is gearing your daily performance to the whims of what someone else wants in order to provide them with a sense that you have accomplished what they would have you to do. You hope that in performing in a certain way, you will earn their approval, a pat on the head, or their love. I told a friend of mine about performance love and he laughed and said, "I ain't in the magic business no more," and that is where you need to get to, my friend – get out of the magic business.

If you see yourself leaving a bad situation, then envision yourself running through that open door, getting out of that space or situation. If you envision yourself buying a new house, then envision yourself signing the mortgage and getting the keys. If you are going to dream, dream *big* my friend!

In the space below list the components of your vision:

1. _____
2. _____
3. _____

"Formulate and stamp an indelible mental picture of yourself succeeding. Hold this picture tenaciously. Never permit it to fade. Your mind will seek to develop the picture... do not build up obstacles in your imagination." - Norman Vincent Peale

Power Tool
Visualization Picture Board

Cut out pictures from magazines, newspapers, and from the internet that are what you envision yourself doing and paste or tape them in the spaces below. Review these pictures daily.
#PowerTools4Success

Power Tool 4
Patience

PATIENCE: Endurance, fortitude, stoicism, persistent courage in trying circumstances.

In discovering what **inhibits** your **patience,** it would be wise to understand this lesson from Machiavelli: "For among other evils caused by being disarmed, it renders you contemptible; which is one of those disgraceful things which a prince must guard against." We should keep this lesson in mind particularly as we seek to uncover the **patience inhibitors** that confront us on a daily basis.

In the space below I would like for you to list the things that test your strength, staying power and calmness:

(1)_____, (2) _____, (3) _____

Remember, you are dealing with people and some **patience inhibitors** are driven by the human need to achieve at your expense. Call it whatever you want but face it – some people just flat out do not want to see you succeed. It is important for you to understand what motivates people who seek your destruction.

You may be thinking, "It ain't that deep," but I will say to you it is deeper than you have fooled yourself to believe.

Do not allow yourself to be lulled into a false sense of security regarding your forward progress. I am a man of faith and in the years leading up to me finally writing this workbook, there is one Scripture that I held on to:

"[12] Not that I have already attained, or am already perfected; but I press on, that I may lay hold of that for which Christ Jesus has also laid hold of me. [13] Brethren, I do not count myself to have apprehended; but one thing I do, forgetting those things which are behind and reaching forward to those things which are ahead, [14] I press toward the goal for the prize of the upward call of God in Christ Jesus." – Philippians 3:12-14 (NKJV)

I urge you to use this time to discover your **patience inhibitors** and I guarantee you that when you understand what they are, you will catapult yourself forward into the life of your dreams.

Power Tool 4
Patience Igniters

Let's focus on the things that **ignite** your **patience**. What are those intangible things that push you forward, or make you feel strong? "Patience is not the ability to wait. Patience is to be calm no matter what happens, constantly take action to turn it to positive growth opportunities and have faith to believe that it will all work out in the end while you are waiting." - Roy T. Bennett

What are three **patience igniters** you rely on for calmness and stability when all odds seem stacked against you? List them below:

1. _____
2. _____
3. _____

Find your place of calmness and persistent courage and hold on – you are on the right path. Obstacles and distractions may appear but stay encouraged. Now that you are aligning with your calling and your purpose, nothing can stop you now. Dear friend, remain strong, smart and courageous.

#PowerTools4Success

Power Tool 4
Patience Action Plan

Patience is a virtue that must be developed. What three actions can you undertake over the next 21 days to become more patient about your success? Make a plan to learn patience and the different effects that it can have on your life and relationships. **#PowerTools4Success**

Actions	Commitment
<u>Goals Set</u>	What books will you read? What newspapers will read? Will you become a blogger?
<u>New Learning</u>	What podcast will you listen to? What webinars will you watch and participate? What podcast will you host?
<u>Relationships</u>	What networking functions will you attend? Who do you need to meet for new business? What new positive and productive people will you meet? Can you grow any current relationships?

Power Tool
Believe

Find something to believe in. I believe in the life, death, burial and resurrection of Jesus Christ. I don't know who you are and where you are, but something led you to this workbook. I strongly encourage you to find something to believe in greater than yourself, but the choice is yours.

I could write for days on end about why you should choose one religion, culture, or form of belief over another but that is not the purpose of this section. The purpose of this section is to persuade you not to choose the route of "rugged individualism" – *the belief that all individuals, or nearly all individuals, can succeed on their own.* You and I both know that we have been using rugged individualism in a much different way than the stated definition; our application of rugged individualism probably sounds more like ***I can make it on my own and I don't need anyone's help.***

Let me say this to you; that is a lie from the pit of hell. You cannot do what needs to be done, you cannot get to where you need to go, and you cannot fight all the fights that need to be fought by yourself. Period. No one does anything great alone; everybody needs help sometimes. Get yourself some friends who love you and are not afraid of you. Whatever you do, do not do it alone because there is nothing to being alone but being lonely. **#PowerTools4Success**

Power Tool
You Need to Get

I have realized that there are a few things that I must have in my life. Below, I list the things that I need for my happiness and I would like for you to create your list of what you need to be happy. Send me a copy and let's talk about your list at ***mcpowertools@gmail.com.***

The *You Need to Get You* List

My List	**Your List**
1. Friends who are not afraid of you	1.
2. Get over yourself	2.
3. Discipline	3.
4. Being fit	4.
5. A hobby	5.
6. An accountability partner	6.

Life is short, but once you decide to live, your world will open. My friends, start living and don't look back!

Power Tool 5
Perseverance

PERSEVERANCE: Steady persistence in a course of action in spite of difficulties, obstacles, or discouragement.

Some people just quit on themselves and maybe there are people who have given up on you, but don't you ever give up on yourself! I have concluded that the only way to win in this life is not to quit. I believe that we must move forward each day, and even on those days when we have more quit than fight within us, we must move forward towards something.

No matter what you are going through in your life at this moment, find a place to go each day. **DO NOT** stay in that apartment or house another day. You are a powerful, gifted, skillful and a proud person capable of great things, but you must seek what is out there in the world for you to do. "The only thing that comes to a sleeper is a dream," so stop dreaming about what was or what could have been and create your new reality.

What **inhibits** perseverance? When I was going through a rough patch, my father once asked me, "Have you ever seen a dog bark at a parked car?" I answered, "No. I have only seen dogs chasing and barking at cars that are moving and going in one direction or another." He said, "That's right, son. Dogs only bark at cars that are moving." So, let the dogs in your life keep on barking at you because if you were sitting still and not growing or going somewhere, you would not hear from them at all.

Dear friend, remain steadfast and immovable from your path. **Do not get off this path you are on**. I highly recommend that you continue to let the dogs of your life bark at you as you pass them by. Keep moving forward, keep moving up, and keep growing.

Finally, let the words of Beyonce marinate in your spirit for just a little while, "I'ma keep running cause a winner don't quit on themselves.

Power Tool 5
Perseverance Inhibitors

Surely, there is enough going on in your world that would make an ordinary man or woman quit, but there is nothing ordinary about you. You are extraordinary and there is no one else like you in creation. Quitting is not an option for you.

When you think of the people who have persevered in the face of great challenges, it is important that you try to adopt some of the traits they displayed on their way to victory:

1. Thomas Edison: Edison is famous for saying that genius is **"1% inspiration and 99% perspiration."**
2. Simon Cowell, the producer of American Idol, had his own publishing company, E&S, and it closed in its first year. Cowell ended up with a lot of debt and was forced to move back in with his parents. However, he never gave up on his dream of working in the music industry.

Perseverance inhibitors: List three reasons for you to **persevere** against difficulties, obstacles, and discouragement. Complete the three sentences below:

1. I will use **"1% inspiration and 99% perspiration"** to:

   _____

   _____

2. I will **never give up**:

   _____

   _____

3. I will **get up and go back**:

   _____

   _____

My hope for you is that you write them not only on this page but also on your heart and mind. No matter how impossible the odds may appear against you, these will be the reasons that will give you encouragement to move onward.

Power Tool 5
Perseverance • Workspace

In the space below, write all that you have overcome. Use what you have written as a reminder of just how far you have come.

_____
_____
_____
_____
_____
_____
_____
_____
_____
_____
_____
_____
_____
_____
_____
_____
_____
_____
_____
_____
_____
_____
_____
_____
_____
_____
_____

Power Tool 5
Perseverance • The Finish Line

Our race has just begun, but the purpose of this page is for you to visualize your future, how you feel, who you'll be with, and what you will have accomplished by getting to your new reality. Far too many people have no idea where they are going, what will be required to get there, and what they will feel along the way, but I declare that you and I will not have those concerns. All obstacles that appear on our paths will be no more than boulders that need to be crushed by the might of our hammers! Mountains will turn into mere dust as we trample them under our feet! Oh, how sore your cheeks will feel from smiling that great victory smile ear to ear when we cross the finish line!

Who	Feel	What

Our race has just begun! The purpose of this page is for you to visualize your future, how you feel, who you'll be with, and what you will have accomplished by getting to your new reality.

You have had time to think, write, plan, and visualize your new reality. Now it is time to go and make it happen. As you go forward, I leave you with this:

> **There is only one you and there will never be another. Do not allow yourself to be constrained, controlled or manipulated by those who have no interest in your success. You must take and maintain control of your emotions and your mind. Those are the only things that you can control. Fight as if your life depended upon maintaining control over both because it does.**

#PowerTools4Success

Dear Friend:

Creation is waiting on you, your gifts, and your power. You have been holding back for too long, so don't make us wait any longer for your arrival!

I am here for you and available to respond to your email at *mcpowertools@gmail.com.*

#PowerTools4Success

Mark Corbin

"I'm becoming more than I have ever been."

· Mark Corbin ·

BONUS CONTENT

Power Tools Weekly Planner 2020
Week 1

The Reconstruction of You:
Utilize this time as the year begins, to create new structures for your life. My guess, is that you do not need to change your whole being, but there are some changes you have been wanting to make regarding how you do things, the way you think and the way in which you manage and maintain your relationships. Start today! List the changes that you want to make and gradually make those changes over the next 365 days. I want to stay connected to you! Let me know your progress and if you find yourself stuck, reach out to me via email.

The Changes: In the spaces below, list what it is you would like to change about you:

1._____

2._____

3._____

Improve your physical fitness: Exercise daily; work a muscle group each day utilizing Yoga or body weight movements. Keep in mind the following:
1. Isometric moves at your desk during the workday;
2. get off the elevator 2-floors below your designation and walk up.

Need help? Contact Personal Trainer, Vernell Bailey at: baileyvernell40@gmail.com.

What fun will you have this year?
_____

_____

_____

Send me an email and let me know what you try this year for FUN!

"Reading is Fundamental": I suggest you read 12 books this year. I suggest the following:
1. *Unbroken* by Laura Hillenbrand
2. *Do the Work* by Steven Pressfield
3. *Standing at the Scratch Line* by Guy Johnson.

I would love to see your reading list for 2020. Send me a few suggestions at my email.

List of things to consider for 2020:
1. Make one new friend;
2. Strengthen love relationships
3. Learn a new skill;
4. Write an E-book;
5. Volunteer.

What does your list contain? Send me a copy at my email and let's compare notes!

Do something that you have always wanted to do in 2020. Share your ideas with me, via email.

What things you have been putting off:

1._____

2. _____

3._____

Review your Life List© and beware of your of Inhibiters.

"Ye shall not fear them: for the Lord your God shall fight for you." – Deuteronomy 3:22

Power Tools Weekly Planner 2020

How are You?
You have made a lot of plans as we have moved away from the light and trite New Year's resolutions. This is the year we get things done. The key is achieving DAILY victories. We are not in the business of saving the world this year. We are in the business of self-care, improving our lives by setting goals and smashing them. You have done your homework and chosen your goals wisely. You will achieve lasting change! If you get frustrated or stuck, reach out to me mcpowertoolss@gmail.com. You are not alone.

What are you feeling: You have made it through the day. Check-in on your emotions and strengths what are you feeling?:

1._____

2._____

3._____

A Key to Improving Your Fitness:
Get some rest. One of the most self-destructive habits I developed was falling asleep with the television on. Turn the television off and get some rest.

What are your fun goals this year?

1. _____

2. _____

3. _____

Let me know what you try this year for fun! mcpowertools@gmail.com

#PowerTools4Success

"Reading is Fundamental": I suggested three books to you earlier which book did you choose? _____

My first choice, **_Do the Work_** by Steven Pressfield. Let me know your choice at mcpowertools@gmail.com

List of things to consider for 2020:
1. Make one new friend;
2. Strengthen love relationships;
3. Learn a new skill;
4. Write an E-book;
5. Volunteer

What does your list contain? Send me a copy at my email, and let's compare notes!

Do something that you have always wanted to do in 2020. Send me an email and share your ideas!

List the things you have been putting off. Now let's go get them:

1. _____

2. _____

3. _____

Review your Life List © and beware of your of Inhibitors.

Power Tools Weekly Planner 2020

Daily Activity	Time	Daily Activity	Time
	6:00am 6:30am		1:00pm 1:30pm
	7:00am 7:30am		2:00pm 2:30pm
	8:00am 8:30am		3:00pm 3:30pm
	9:00am 9:30am		4:00pm 4:30pm
	10:00am 10:30am		5:00pm 5:30pm
	11:00am 11:30am		6:00pm 6:30pm
	12:00pm 12:30pm		7:00pm 7:30pm

Note: New or additional thoughts should be recorded on your mobile phone recorder or leave a message for yourself in your voice mail. This should alleviate forgetting future tasks, assignments and appointments.

Daily S.M.A.R.T. Goals: Specific: What, Why, and How, **Measurable:** Measure it, you can't manage it, **Attainable:** What do you want, **Realistic:** Doable and **Timely:** Specific timeframe for achieving your goal:

1._____
2._____
3._____

Daily Inhibitors

1. _____
2. _____
3. _____

Person you need to meet this week who can help your life, business or education grow?
1._____

Daily Igniters

1. _____
2. _____
3. _____

Next Day Goals

1. _____
2. _____
3. _____

Daily Victory:_____

Your number 1 goal each day is to win! Create situations for yourself each day. The best way to do this is to think and act S.M.A.R.T.

Power Tools Weekly Planner 2020

Daily Update

_____
_____
_____
_____
_____
_____
_____
_____

Task: (*Including new or unexpected*)
1._____

2._____

3._____

New Connections: (who did you meet)
1._____

2._____

3._____

What did you learn today?
1._____

2._____

3._____

How did you take care of your body, mind and spirit today?
1._____

2._____

3._____

Begin Now!

Positive Self-Talk: (What did you tell yourself today?)
_____
_____
_____

Power Tools Weekly Planner 2020

Daily Update

_____
_____
_____
_____
_____
_____
_____
_____
_____

Task: (*Including new or unexpected*)
1._____
2._____
3._____

New Connections: (who did you meet)
1._____
2._____
3._____

What did you learn today?
1._____
2._____
3._____

How did you take care of your body, mind and spirit today?
1._____
2._____
3._____

Begin Now!

Positive Self-Talk: (What did you tell yourself today?)
_____
_____
_____

Power Tools Weekly Planner 2020
Week 2

The Reconstruction of You:
Utilize this time as the year begins, to create new structures for your life. My guess, is that you do not need to change your whole being, but there are some changes you have been wanting to make regarding how you do things, the way you think and the way in which you manage and maintain your relationships. Start today! List the changes that you want to make and gradually make those changes over the next 365 days. I want to stay connected to you! Let me know your progress and if you find yourself stuck, reach out to me via email.

The Changes: In the spaces below, list what it is you would like to change about you:

1._____

2._____

3._____

Improve your physical fitness: Exercise daily; work a muscle group each day utilizing Yoga or body weight movements. Keep in mind the following:
1. Isometric moves at your desk during the workday;
2. get off the elevator 2-floors below your designation and walk up.

Need help? Contact Personal Trainer, Vernell Bailey at: baileyvernell40@gmail.com.

What fun will you have this year?

_____

_____

_____

Send me an email and let me know what you try this year for FUN!

"Reading is Fundamental": I suggest you read 12 books this year. I suggest the following:
4. *<u>Unbroken</u>* by Laura Hillenbrand
5. *<u>Do the Work</u>* by Steven Pressfield
6. *<u>Standing at the Scratch Line</u>* by Guy Johnson.

I would love to see your reading list for 2020. Send me a few suggestions at my email.

List of things to consider for 2020:
6. Make one new friend;
7. Strengthen love relationships
8. Learn a new skill;
9. Write an E-book;
10. Volunteer.

What does your list contain? Send me a copy at my email and let's compare notes!

Do something that you have always wanted to do in 2020. Share your ideas with me, via email.

What things you have been putting off:

1._____

2. _____

3._____

Review your Life List© and beware of your of Inhibiters.

"The Lord is my rock and my fortress and my deliverer, my God, my strength in whom I will trust. My shield and the horn of my salvation, my stronghold." – Psalms 18:2

Power Tools Weekly Planner 2020

How are You?
You have made a lot of plans as we have moved away from the light and trite New Year's resolutions. This is the year we get things done. The key is achieving DAILY victories. We are not in the business of saving the world this year. We are in the business of self-care, improving our lives by setting goals and smashing them. You have done your homework and chosen your goals wisely. You will achieve lasting change! If you get frustrated or stuck, reach out to me mcpowertoolss@gmail.com. You are not alone.

What are you feeling: You have made it through the day. Check-in on your emotions and strengths what are you feeling?:

1._____

2._____

3._____

A Key to Improving Your Fitness:
Get some rest. One of the most self-destructive habits I developed was falling asleep with the television on. Turn the television off and get some rest.

What are your fun goals this year?

1. _____

2. _____

3. _____

Let me know what you try this year for fun! mcpowertools@gmail.com

#PowerTools4Success

"Reading is Fundamental": I suggested three books to you earlier which book did you choose? _____

My first choice, **_Do the Work_** by Steven Pressfield. Let me know your choice at mcpowertools@gmail.com

List of things to consider for 2020:

6. Make one new friend;
7. Strengthen love relationships;
8. Learn a new skill;
9. Write an E-book;
10. Volunteer

What does your list contain? Send me a copy at my email, and let's compare notes!

Do something that you have always wanted to do in 2020. Send me an email and share your ideas!

List the things you have been putting off. Now let's go get them:

3. _____

2. _____

3. _____

Review your Life List © and beware of your of Inhibitors.

Power Tools Weekly Planner 2020

Daily Activity	Time	Daily Activity	Time
	6:00am 6:30am		1:00pm 1:30pm
	7:00am 7:30am		2:00pm 2:30pm
	8:00am 8:30am		3:00pm 3:30pm
	9:00am 9:30am		4:00pm 4:30pm
	10:00am 10:30am		5:00pm 5:30pm
	11:00am 11:30am		6:00pm 6:30pm
	12:00pm 12:30pm		7:00pm 7:30pm

Note: New or additional thoughts should be recorded on your mobile phone recorder or leave a message for yourself in your voice mail. This should alleviate forgetting future tasks, assignments and appointments.

Daily S.M.A.R.T. Goals: Specific: What, Why, and How, **Measurable:** Measure it, you can't manage it, **Attainable:** What do you want, **Realistic:** Doable and **Timely:** Specific timeframe for achieving your goal:

1._____
2._____
3._____

Daily Inhibitors
1. _____
2. _____
3. _____

Person you need to meet this week who can help your life, business or education grow?
1._____

Daily Igniters
1. _____
2. _____
3. _____

Next Day Goals
1. _____
2. _____
3. _____

Daily Victory: _____

Your number one goal each day is to win! Create situations for yourself each day. The best way to do this is to think and act S.M.A.R.T.

Power Tools Weekly Planner 2020

Daily Update

_____
_____
_____
_____
_____
_____
_____
_____
_____

Task: (*Including new or unexpected*)
1. _____
2. _____
3. _____

New Connections: (who did you meet)
1. _____
2. _____
3. _____

What did you learn today?
1. _____
2. _____
3. _____

How did you take care of your body, mind and spirit today?
1. _____
2. _____
3. _____

Begin Now!

Positive Self-Talk: (What did you tell yourself today?)

_____
_____
_____

Power Tools Weekly Planner 2020

Daily Update

_____
_____
_____
_____
_____
_____
_____
_____

Task: (*Including new or unexpected*)

1._____

2._____

3._____

New Connections: (who did you meet)

1._____

2._____

3._____

What did you learn today?

1._____

2._____

3._____

How did you take care of your body, mind and spirit today?

1._____

2._____

3._____

Begin Now!

Positive Self-Talk: (What did you tell yourself today?)

_____
_____
_____

Notes:

Sources:

1. SMART Goal Setting: A Surefire Way To Achieve Your Goals; http://www.goal-setting-guide.com/goal-setting-tutorials/smart-goal-setting ; by Arina February 20, 2010
2. Psalm 31:24 (NKJV); http://www.biblegateway.com/
3. Norman Vincent Peale Quotes: http://www.brainyquote.com/quotes/authors/n/norman_vincent_peale.html
4. Vince Lombardi Quote: http://www.successories.com/iquote/author/2671/vince-lombardi-quotes/1
5. Winston Churchill Quotes:
6. http://www.brainyquote.com/quotes/authors/w/winston_churchill.html
7. Indira Gandhi Quote:; http://www.brainyquote.com/quotes/authors/i/indira_gandhi.html
8. Tom Landry Quotes: http://www.brainyquote.com/quotes/authors/t/tom_landry.html
9. John F. Kennedy Quote: http://www.brainyquote.com/quotes/authors/j/john_f_kennedy.html
10. Abraham Lincoln Quote: http://www.brainyquote.com/quotes/authors/a/abraham_lincoln.html
11. Sun Tzu Quote: http://www.brainyquote.com/quotes/authors/s/sun_tzu.html
12. Fit Definition; https://www.google.com/search
13. Cowardly Lion Speech: http://www.americanrhetoric.com/MovieSpeeches/moviespeechthewizardofozcourage.html
14. Niccolo Machiavelli Quote; http://www.brainyquote.com/quotes/authors/n/niccolo_machiavelli.html#9fCuLG1sg8IGmuUJ.99
15. Philippians 3:11-21 (NKJV): http://www.biblegateway.com/
16. Rudyard Kipling, If; http://allspirit.co.uk/kipling.html
17. Master Mind Group definition: http://www.thesuccessalliance.com/what-is-a-mastermind-group.html
18. Thomas Edison and Simone Cowell information: http://www.growthink.com/content/7-entrepreneurs-whose-perseverance-will-inspire-you
19. Romans 8:18-22; http://www.biblegateway.com/passage/?search=romans%208:18-22&version=NIV
20. Motivation: https://enhancedmotivation.com/movere
21. W. Clement Stone Quote: https://www.brainyquote.com/quotes/w_clement_stone_155728
22. Golda Meir: https://www.brainyquote.com/quotes/golda_meir_162893
23. Ralph Waldo Emerson quote: https://www.goodreads.com/quotes/7966602-what-we-fear-of-doing-most-is-usually-what-we

www.ingramcontent.com/pod-product-compliance
Lightning Source LLC
Chambersburg PA
CBHW040100160426
43193CB00002B/30